# ‘Have YOU Seen My Mojo?’

## and other poems

# author's note

In 2017 at the age of 52, I was diagnosed with Parkinson's disease.

All of the poems in this collection were inspired by my own journey and that of others with Parkinson's disease. They describe my thoughts, feelings and experiences of what it is like to live with an incurable, degenerative neurological condition.

As with all creative writing, a small degree of artistic licence has been employed, since it is hard to find words that rhyme with 'Parkinson's' and 'postural instability'.

# ‘Have YOU Seen My Mojo?’

## and other poems

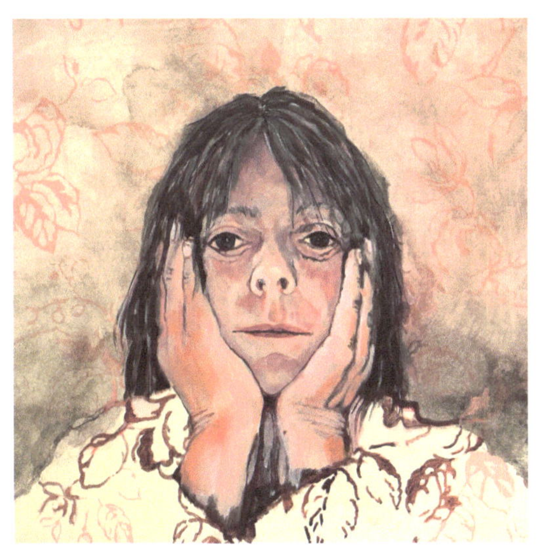

Ali Blevins

First published in Great Britain in 2025



Editing, design, typesetting and publishing by UK Book Publishing.

www.ukbookpublishing.com

ISBN: 978-1-917329-88-0

# contents

# dedication

When you live with a progressive disease that has more than 40 different symptoms, it is easy to slip into the habit of allowing the people around you to do things for you. However, Parkinson's is a disease that thrives on lack of activity, it is so insidious it has even adopted apathy as one of its primary symptoms. For these reasons, with Parkinson's disease, you need to surround yourself with folk who are motivators and who encourage you to do things for yourself.

I call them my 'enablers'.

This book is dedicated to all my enablers. You have been with me, not just on my Parkinson's journey but on my artistic and poetic journey and I could not have created this without your love and support.

This book is also dedicated to anyone recently diagnosed with Parkinson's disease.

I hope you find your enablers.

# introduction

## *creativity*

Scientific evidence suggests, that there is a subset of people, who when treated with dopamine medication for Parkinson's disease, become more creative. My creative output has undoubtedly increased tenfold since diagnosis.

It is an aspect of the disease that can be both rewarding and alarming since the need to create is a compulsion. My friend and fellow poet Nigel Smith described it as 'gentle madness'. I think he could be right.

# diagnosis

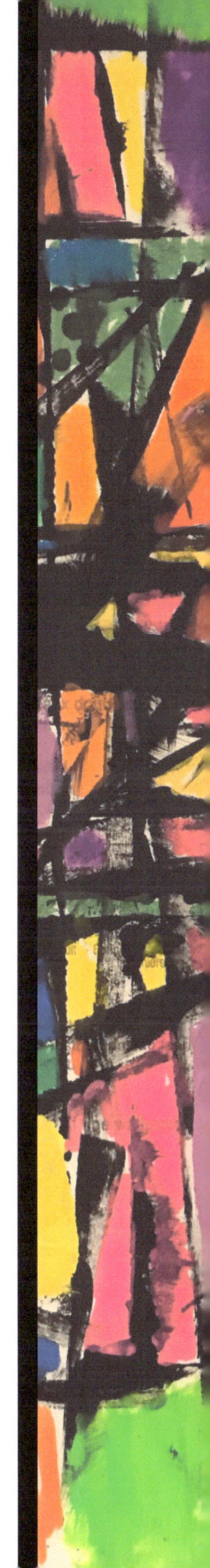

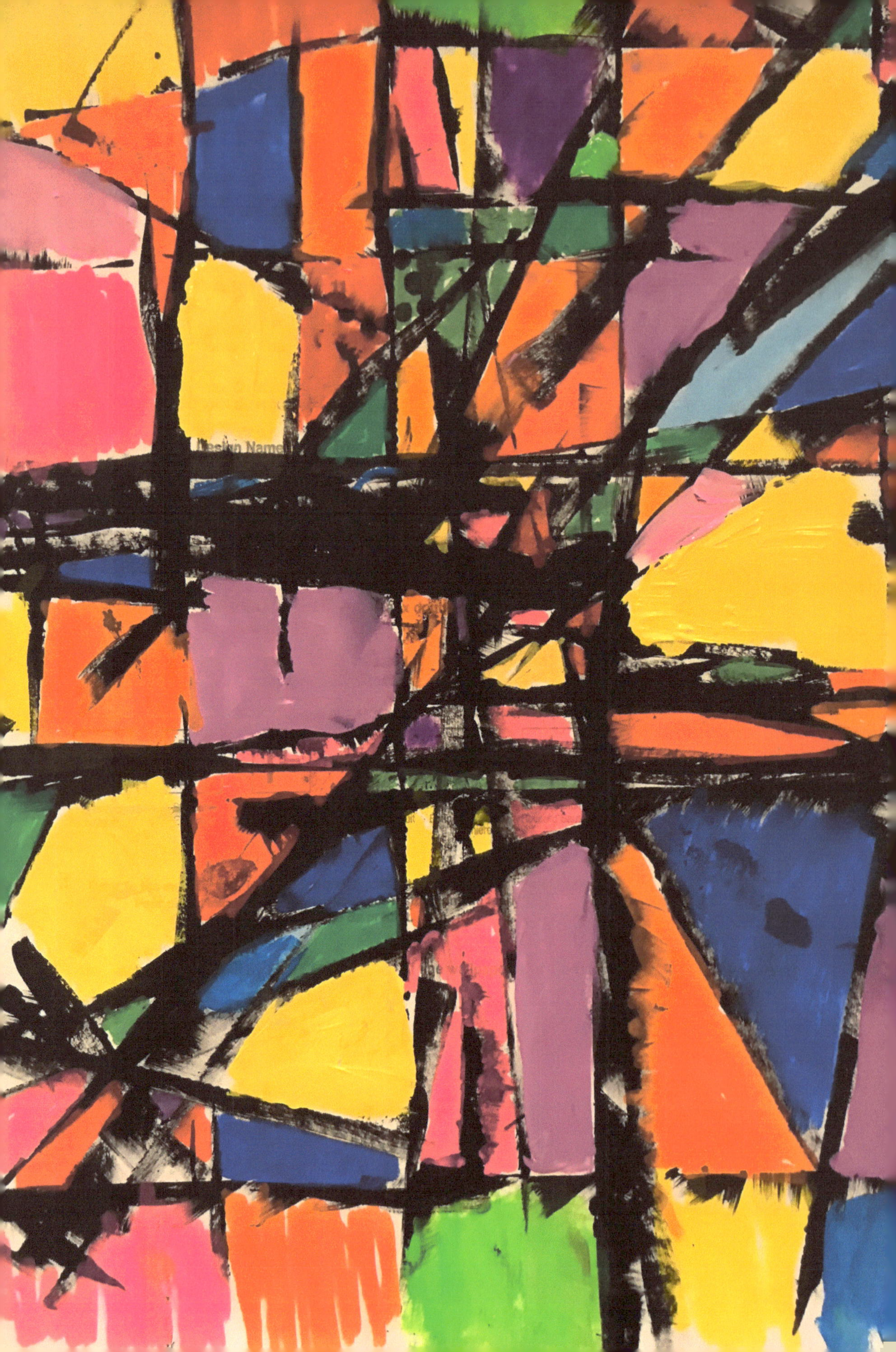

# have you seen my mojo?

Have You Seen My Mojo?
I lost it with, my vibe.
I don't know where I lost it,
it could just be outside.

Or it may be in a pocket
of a jacket, or a coat,
screwed up in a corner
with that note, I wrote.

The note I wrote – to remind me
of all the things that I forget,
like where I put my mojo
I still haven't found it yet.

So, if you find my mojo – please
could you give it back to me,
because without my mojo
I may drown in apathy.

# postural instability

'Don't worry, it won't kill you,'
at least that's what the doctor said,
as if that would make it better –
like – who wants to end up dead?

And it did not make it better,
nor did it put my mind at ease,
this sort of consolation prize –
called Parkinson's disease.

AND besides,

He had paused before he said it,
just enough to make me doubt,
cause a 'teacher-instinct-take-over'
because he'd clearly left things out.

And I knew just what I had to do,
to find out what he wasn't saying.
I had to use my 'teacher eyebrows',
make him explain the game I'm playing.

You see, I rarely ever had to speak
when dishing out my 'teacher rows'.
I could say multitudes,
by simply raising my eyebrows,
for example:

"Stop that now!"
"Put that down!"
"I wouldn't if I were you!"
"Don't take that snack."
"Give it back!"
and
"Do not lick the glue!"

So, I fixed him with my very best –
Paddington-teacher-stare.
I am practised in extracting truth,
lie to me if you dare.

And I made my eyebrows say,
"You know – I know, there's more,"
and reluctantly, he had no choice
but to open up that door.

AND THIS – was his explanation,
of how I won't wind up dead.
Of how Parkinson's won't kill me,
this is what he said:

"Parkinson's disease,
cannot cause death directly.
But if you take a single symptom,
such as, 'postural instability' –

Postural instability causes
an increased risk of falling down.
Therefore, Parkinson's is NOT the cause of death
but your 'head' hitting the ground.

I think it was relief – perhaps?
Since he let out a slightly happy sigh.
But that was before he realised
we were discussing how I'd die.

"I see," I said. But I didn't really,
for once I was struck dumb.
In that moment, I could only feel –
that my eyebrows had gone numb.

And that was it – the big reveal
of what was wrong with me,
and I walked out of his office, but very carefully –
after all, I had to mind 'my postural instability'.

# the appointment

The appointment is at one but I like to be there early,
hand my money to the ticket man, who comes across as surly,
I stare blankly out the window while I contemplate my lot,
'Is this what I was expecting? – No, I think, it's not.'

I watch the trees, the fields, the houses – blurred by the rushing train,
and think about the new stuff, to the doctor, I'll explain.
The little things I'd rather not, to have, to share,
the stuff I try to cover up to keep folk unaware.

And while I'm in the waiting room I play the guessing game –
which of us has Parkinson's, the symptoms are quite plain.
They didn't sign up either, of that I'm pretty sure,
and I wonder, if like me – they were expecting more.

I'm called into a room, asked to take a chair,
"Do I mind if there's a student?" it feels like I'm laid bare.
My mind's unpicked by questions, my symptoms pulled apart,
yet there seem to be no answers, just more notes on my chart.

So, I begin my journey home and the rocking in my brain
co-ordinates itself with the rocking of the train –
it looks like I am dancing to an imaginary song,
there's no point trying to stop it. My only choice – to dance along.

And it would be easy to sink deeper, into the dark pond that is 'Why?'
ignore the brilliant sunshine and the bright blue sky.
To wallow in self-pity, drown in a sea of doubt
but I know this isn't really, what my life's about.

So, as I climb up Trainers Brae, to my house beneath the hill,
I'm aware that bloody Parkinson's remains within me still.
And it will never leave me – it will be there until the end.
I will have to learn to live with it, somehow make it my friend.

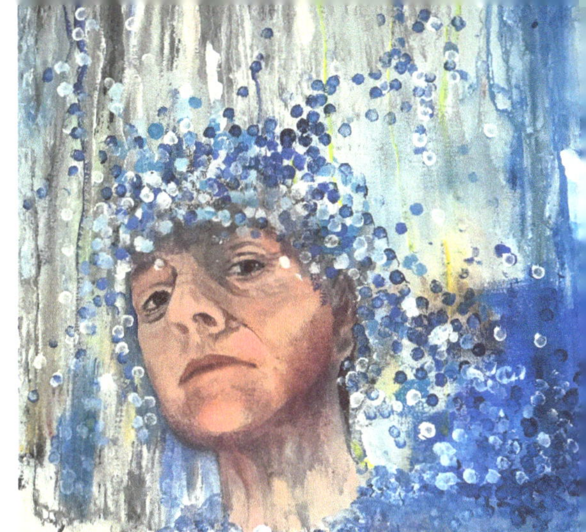

# when?

When was my last unfettered breath?
The one that I took before it began.

Somewhere between an exhale and an inhale –
there was a change. But did I notice?
Did I stop briefly to wonder, 'What just happened?'
Then dismiss it as nothing and carry on.

Was it that time camping in France?
While staring into time-frosted glass, I watched my hand slowly hang
itself.
Suspended in the air – as if caught in a delicate, invisible web.
And I wondered, could that French-speaking spider in the corner have
bewitched me?
So, I asked her,

"Quelle magie as-tu pour me faire ressembler a un cadavre?"

But she did not answer and my fingers fluttered on the toothbrush.
I blamed it on modern comforts.
I was no longer used to such manual labour.
I often wonder when it began.

# coming to terms – or not

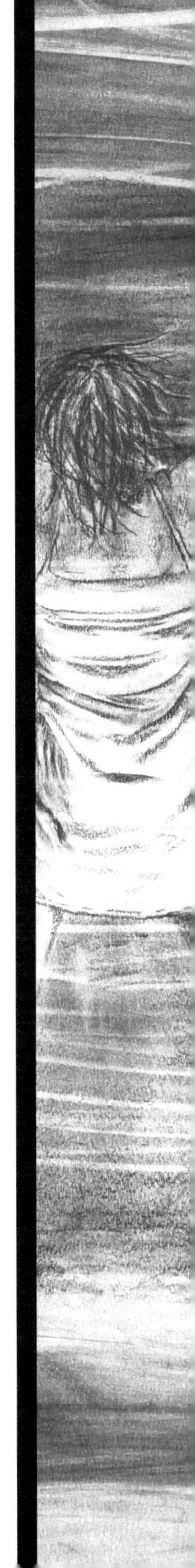

# disappearing

Fading, vanishing, nipped away,
like birds pecking apples.
I was here yesterday. At least –
I thought I was. Now I'm not so sure?
Today I am less. When I thought I was more.

## losing it!

I am spiralling,
spiralling out of control,
spinning, spinning, never winning,
crashing, burning, diving, turning,
falling, dropping, never stopping.

I am losing it!
I am losing
I am losin
I am losi
I am los
I am lo
I am l
I am
I a
I

I
I a
I am
I am lost.

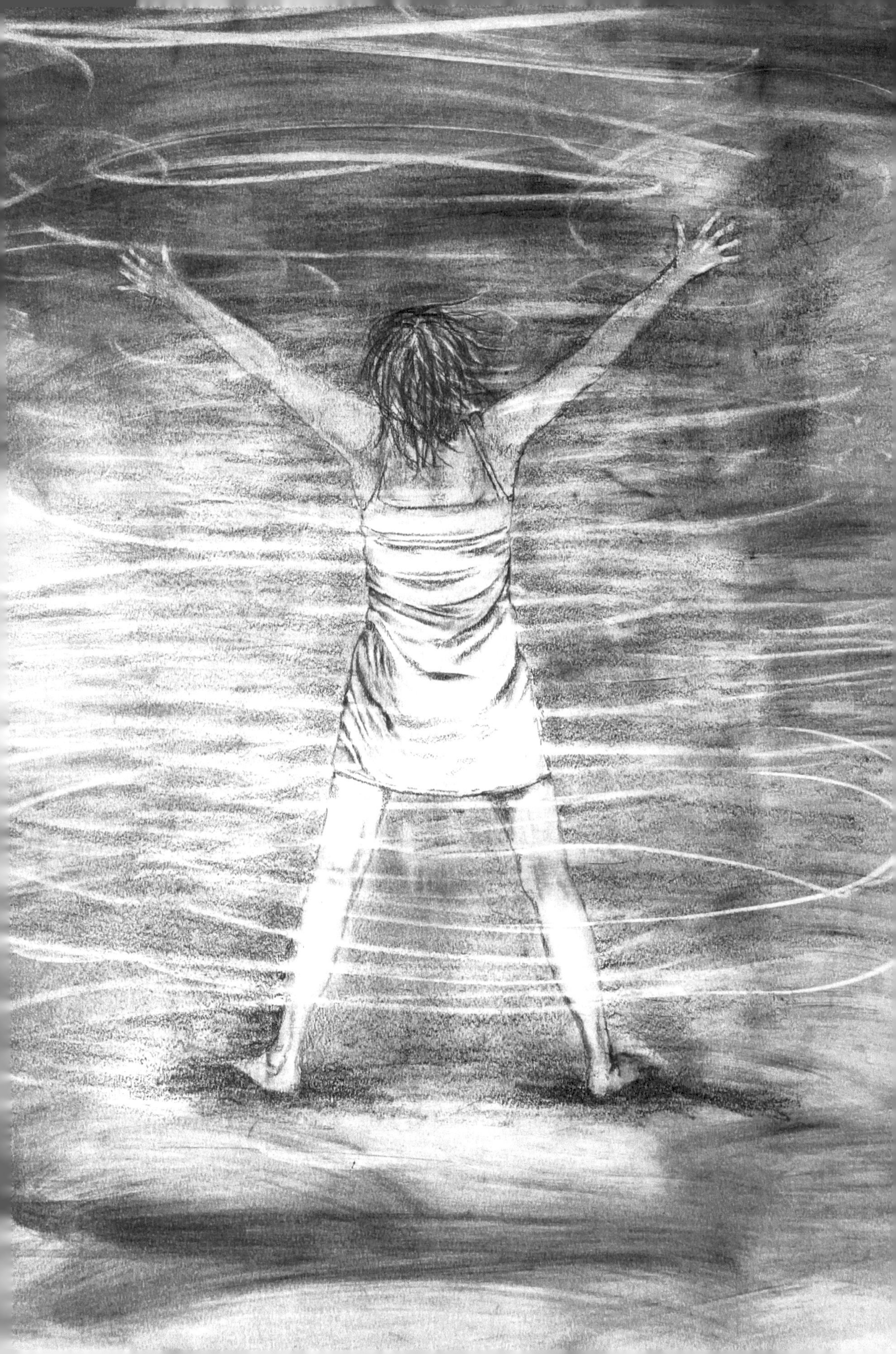

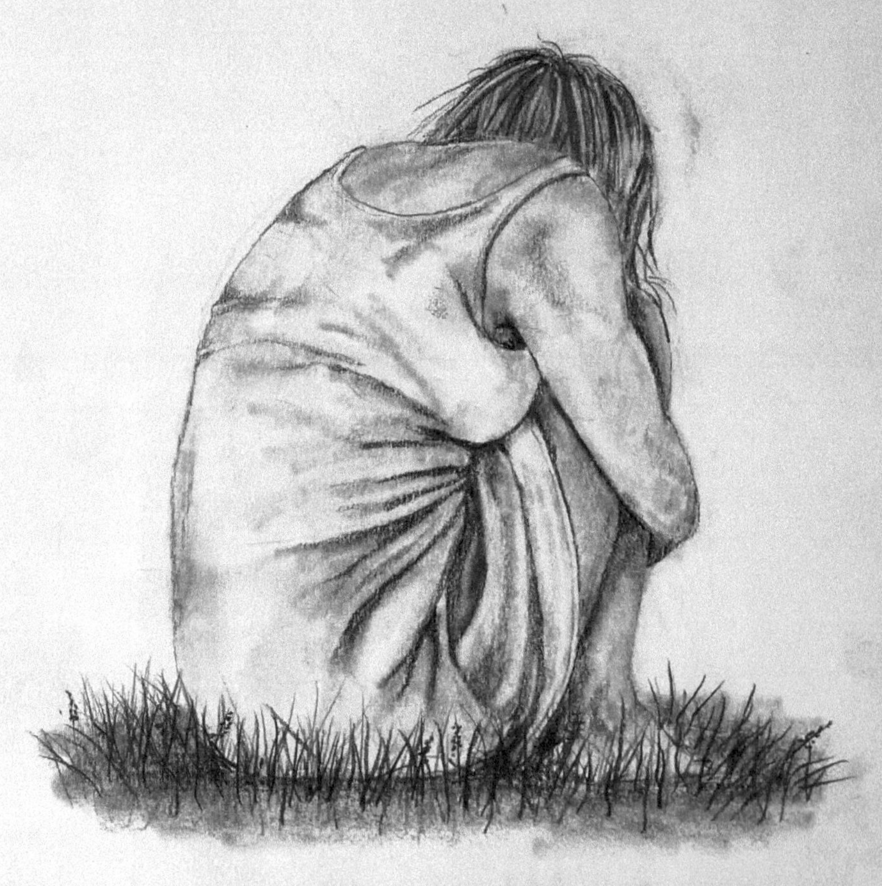

# a place called numb

I am in that place – that numb place.
That place where I am untouchable,
where poking and prodding will merely make dents
in fleshy skin, that slowly rebounds.

I am in that place – that numb place.
That place where time has momentarily stalled
and reality is just a void in which to drop
and never land.

I am in that place – that numb place.
That place where there is no salvation, just medication
and a whole host of side effects
that become mixed up with the disease.

I am in that place – that numb place.
Please understand. I do not choose to be here,
it is not something I planned –
like some sort of holiday.

# some days

Some days I want to curl up small in a ball.
I want to roll up tight, coiled around my soft insides.
I would only offer my back, knees, and elbows to the world.
I would be impenetrable.

Some days I want to howl and yowl like a wolf at the moon.
I want to bellow until my belly bursts and my lungs tear apart.
I want to wail, shriek and screech like a banshee.
I would break the sound barrier with my noise.

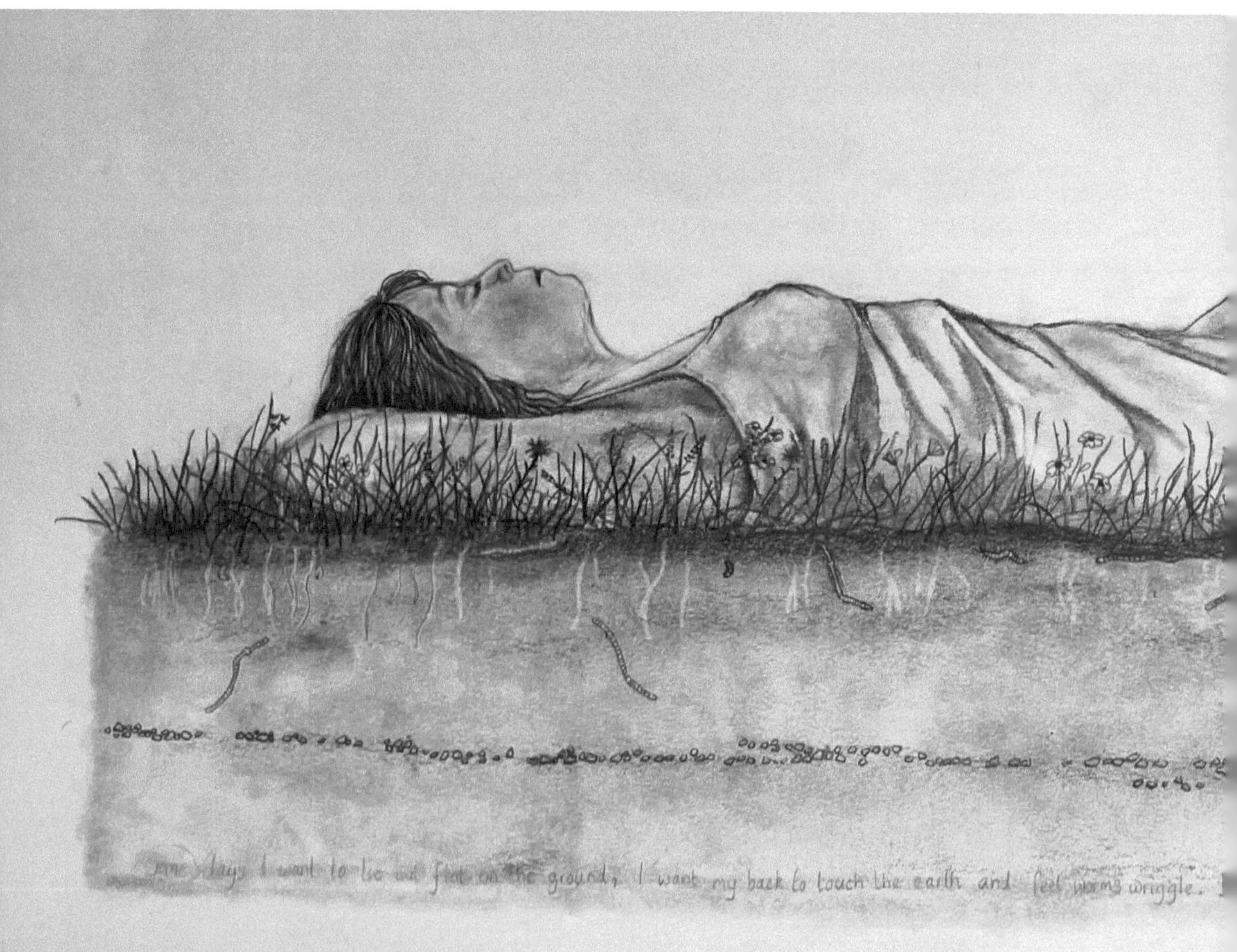

Some days I want like to whirl like a hurricane.
I want to spin faster than the Waltzer at the fair.
I would be a blur of colours, sucking up everything in my path –
And then I would spit out a rainbow.

Some days I want to lie out flat on the ground.
I want my back to touch the earth. I want to feel the worms wriggle.
I would dream of warm summer days and cold winter nights.
And I would be at peace.

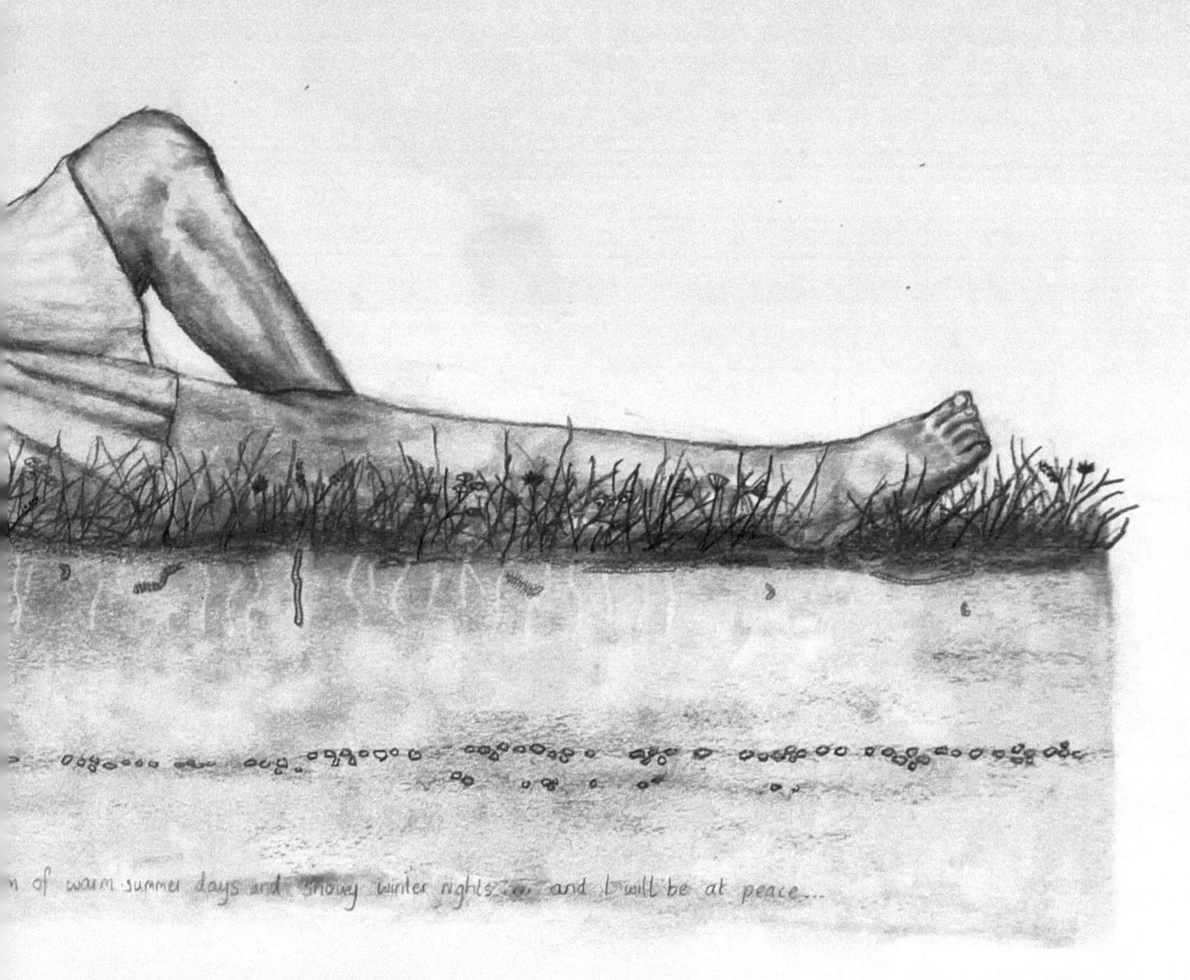

# special gift

There are times,
When this special gift I have been given
I would give it away.
I would give it away.

If I could, I would wrap up tight,
the apathy and anxiety,
the nausea and fatigue,
the stiffness and rigidity,
the cramping and lack of sleep,

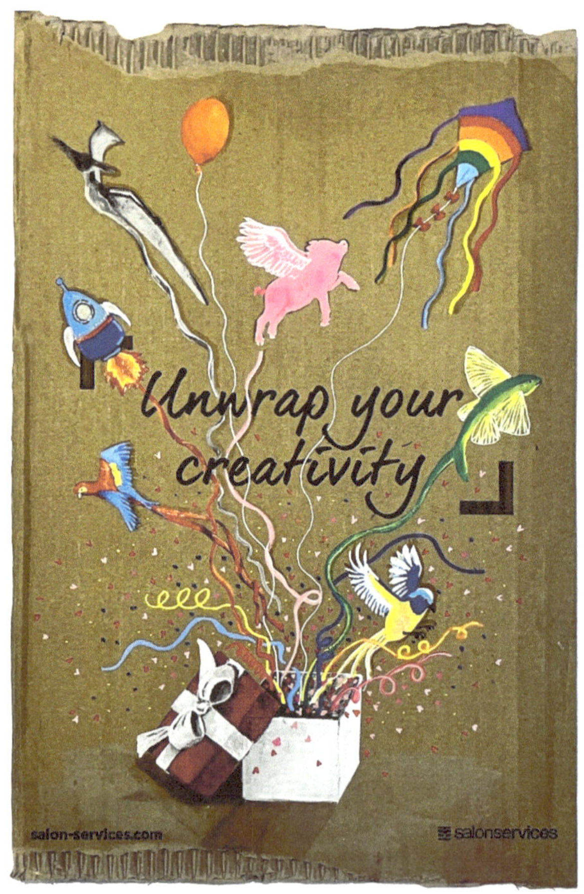

I would wrap it up in tissue and brown paper
and I would give that gift away.

*Or would I?*

To whom could I possibly give this special gift?
My parcel of deceit
I wouldn't wish this special gift on anyone.
I cannot give it away.

Instead? I should kick that parcel as hard as I can.
Make it sky-rocket into space
until it disappears into the stars and is sucked up by a black hole.

*But...*
There is always a 'but'.

There are other times when I open up that parcel – that special gift –
and out spills,
colour,
lines,
shapes,
form
and
a thousand words to describe the world and all its beauty.

And I wonder – If I did kick that gift into the stars.
Would I chase after it?

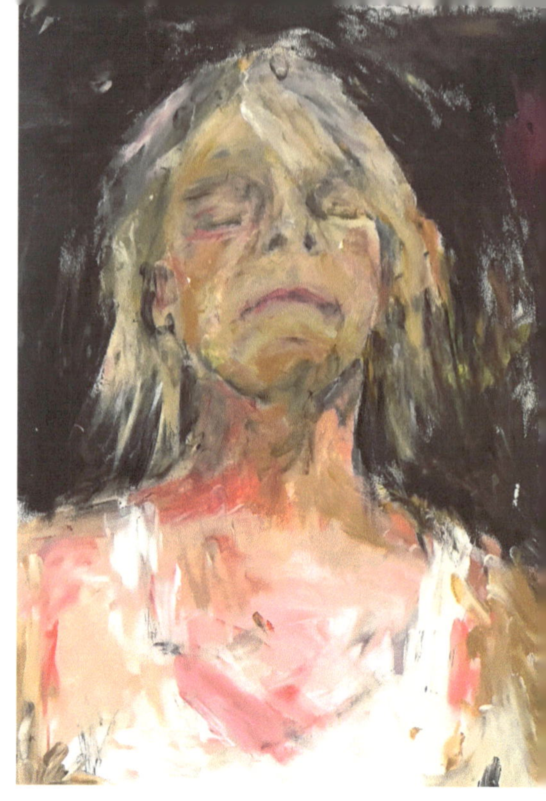

# the real me

When I look in the mirror – I see me
but increasingly I do not recognise
    the woman behind my eyes.

This woman, who is so continuously
    distracted
she is unable to give her full
    attention
to anything or anyone,
even those she loves.

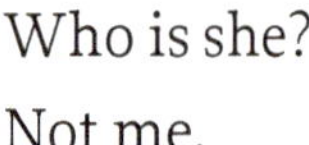

Who is she?
Not me.

Her mind (or is it mine?)
wanders continuously unaware of time,
moving between words and images
that she must play out on a page or a canvas.

Who is she?
Not me.

When I look in the mirror I am scared
that this woman will replace the real me.
The real me, who is slowly disappearing
consumed by a lack of brain cells
and the drugs used to replace them.

When I look in the mirror, I am scared I am becoming only her.
Unable to focus on the here and now of the day
the real me– wants so very much to be present.

So, I search for something that will tether –
the real me to her and her to me –
and I find it in the words and images she wanders through –
the stories she tells, the poems she writes, the pictures she paints. They
reflect who she is and what she loves,

her zest for life
her family
her friends
I know her now.

Who is she?
She is me.

# self portrait

It starts as a want, a need,
an itch that has to be scratched
and then, the rest of the world fades away . . .

Without thinking, 'Am I dressed for this?
Should I be doing something else?'
The clutter is swept away.

Eyes closed – I reach in deep for the bones.
Drawing them to the surface,
tracing their contours
in my mind –
I lay them out upon the canvas.

Millimetre by millimetre,
mark by mark,
I adjust their position and form.
Stroking the canvas until
the briefest elements of life appear.

Mixing Cadmium red and yellow,
a hint of ultramarine blue
I pull flesh from the paint –
round peaches and pinks,
plump reds, sunken purples.

With nuances of colour
I caress her, layer upon layer
until she emerges,
eyes watching me –
asking to be made whole.

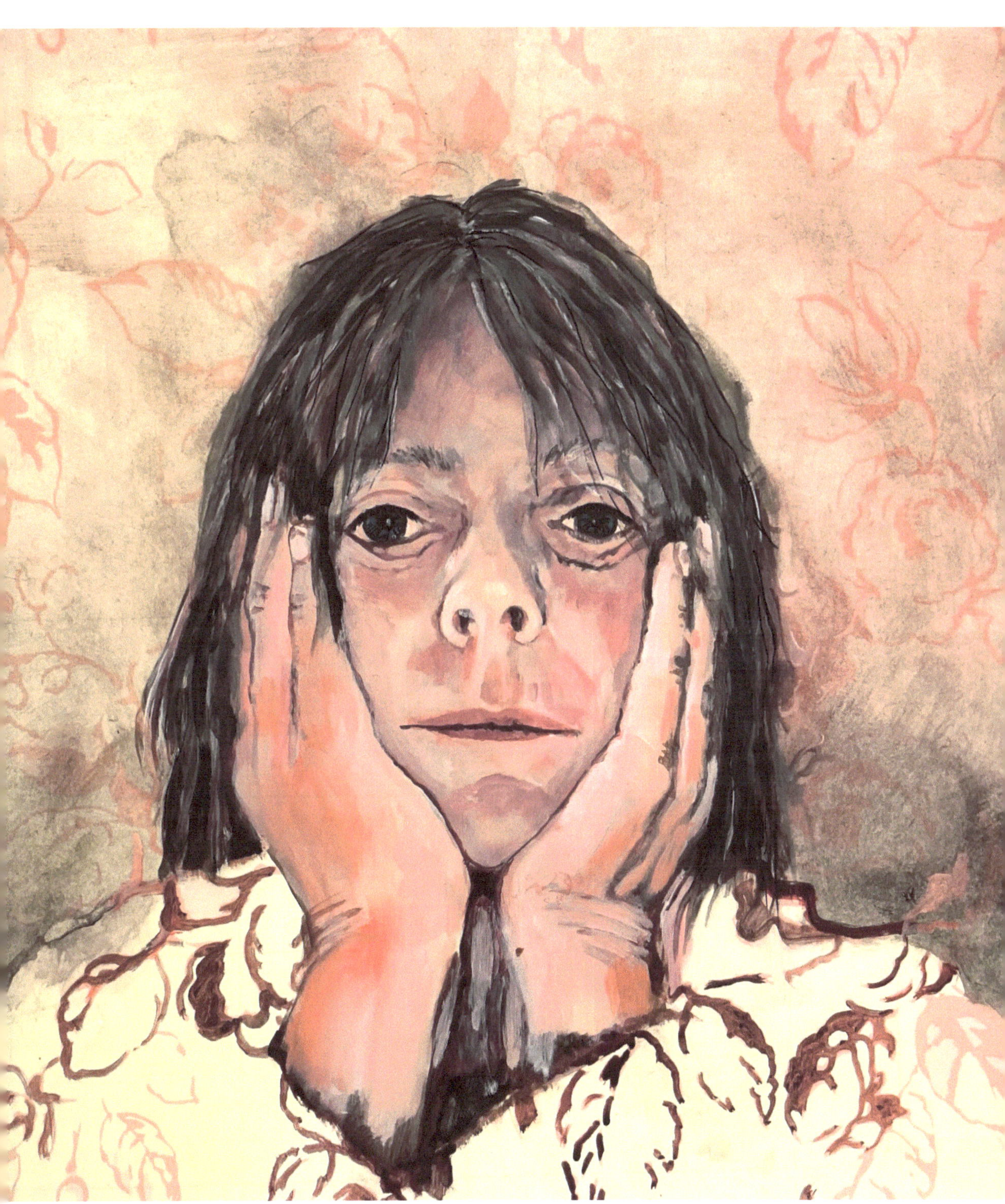

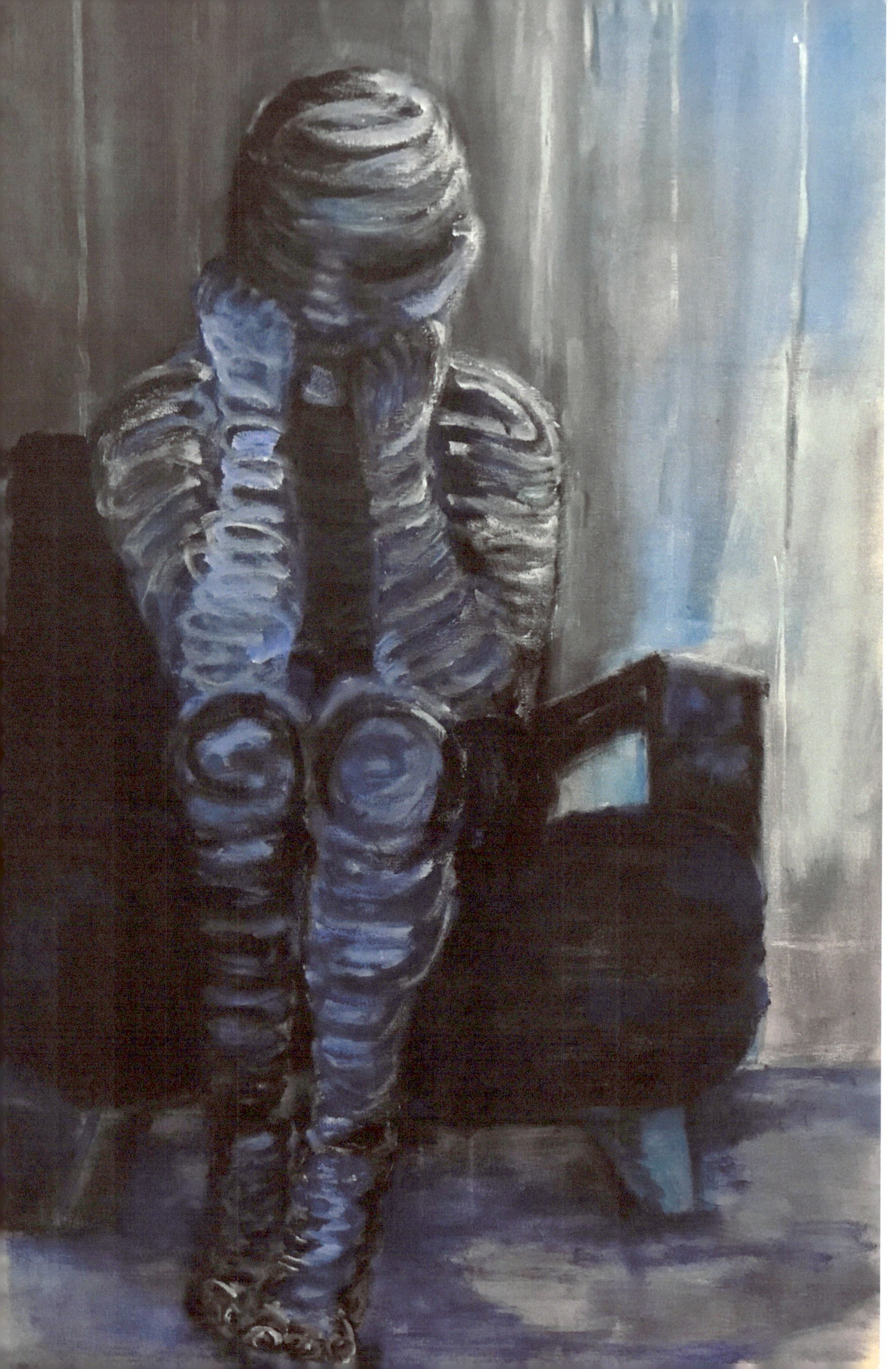

# Frankenstein

Sometimes I feel like Frankenstein
made up of different parts,
at the mercy of a corrupted brain
that works in fits and starts.

So, give me pills and potions
let them work their magic please,
upon my ailing body
and put me at my ease.

Turn me from a lumbering heap
that wobbles when it walks,
that slurs its words and mumbles
every time it talks –

Back into a human being
if only for a while,
so, I can at least walk and talk
with a certain amount of style.

attitude is
everything

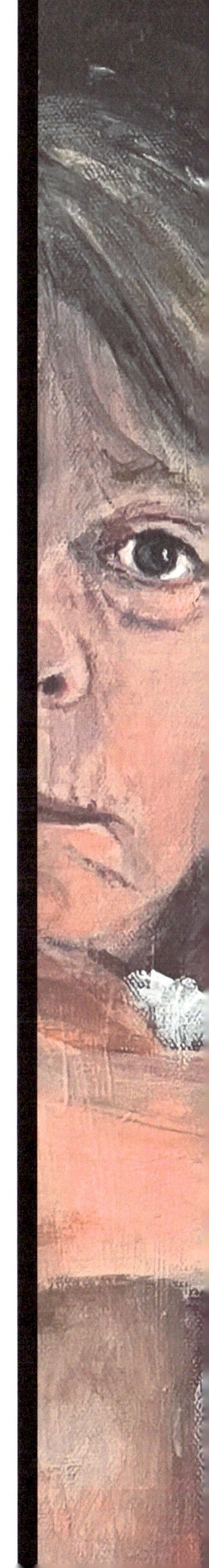

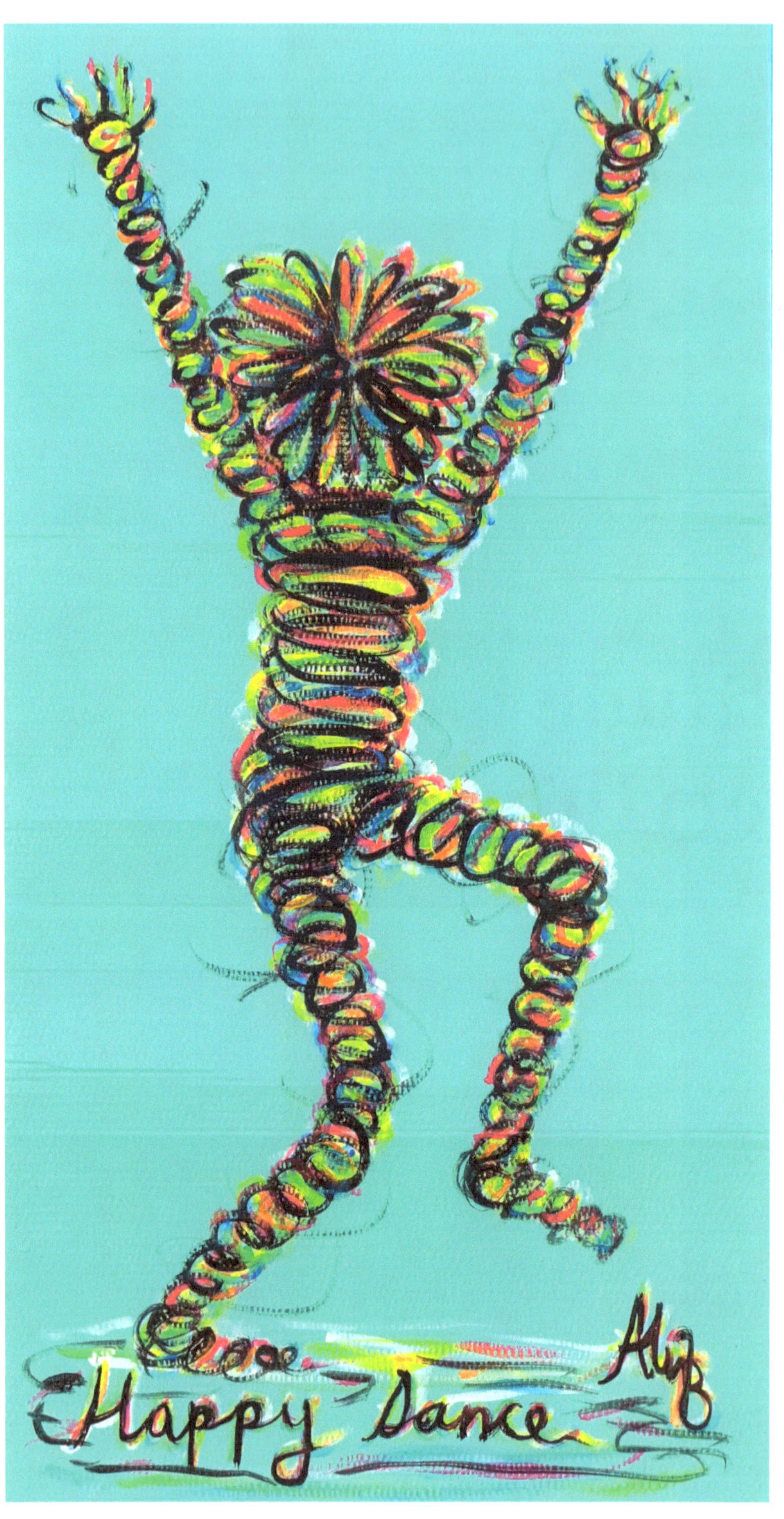
Happy Dance

## attitude

I am 5'2 and a half.
The half is very important –
Attitude is everything.

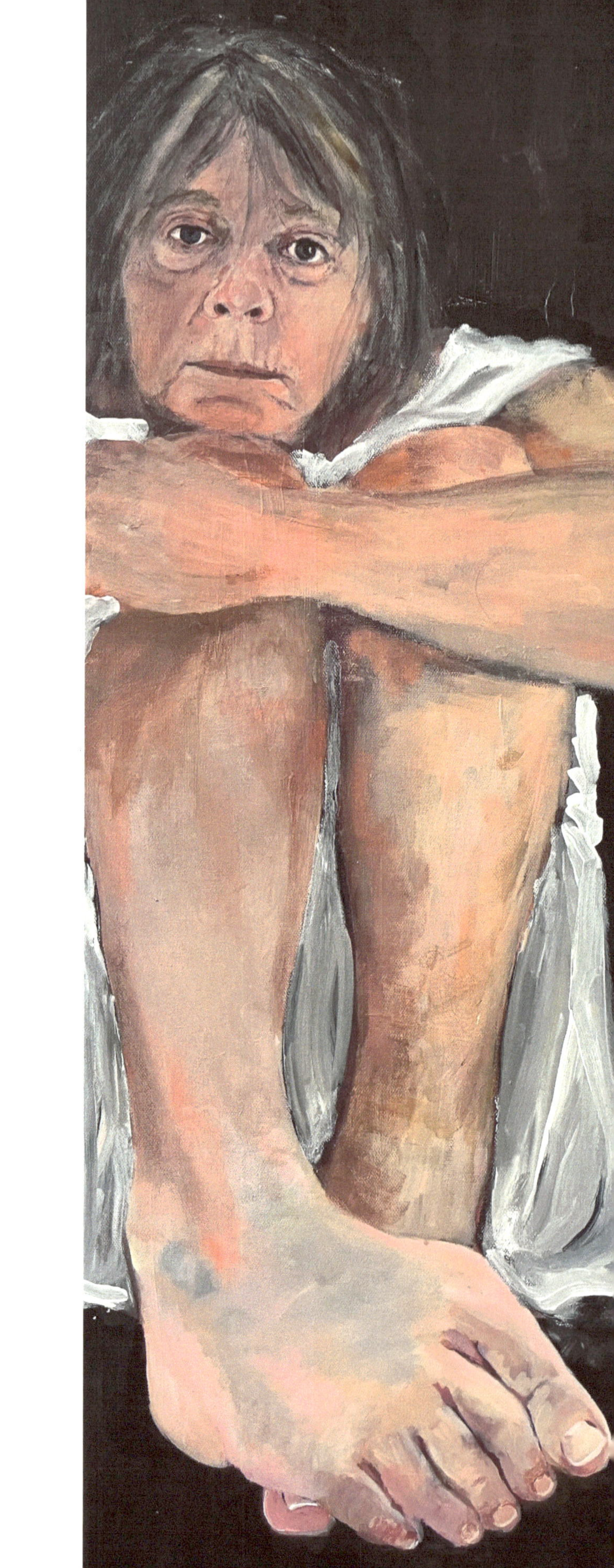

# the losing game

Sometimes although you win a battle,
you know you're going to lose the war
and this game you'll be the loser
even with the highest score.

Sometimes the odds stacked up against you
seem like they're sky-high
and you have lost all sense of happy
you can only question, 'Why?'

Sometimes you long to hide from life,
but you know that will not ease the pain
and the more time that you spend away
just makes it harder to come back again.

So, you must dance your way through darkness
and out the other side,
hitch a ride with 'happiness'
take 'love' along, just for the ride.

And although it's very hard,
this path your life has taken,
with each new day that dawns
it is with hope you must awaken.

## news flash

I knew – when I saw it
I should be filled with hope,
but instead – its guilt-laced dread
and I steel myself to cope
with the flurry of attention –
the messages and texts,
and links embedded in them
to the story they've just read,

(do they think I would have missed it?).

And I'll have to don my armour,
look pleased and paint a smile,
all the while resisting –
the urge to shout, 'It's just a trial!'
Pretending there is hope,
when I know a different truth,
that this (supposed) happy news
is so far very far removed,

from the reality.

I will not receive that lifeline,
(reserved for a selected few).
And I know within my lifetime,
a cure's unlikely too.
So, if I am to survive,
with my sanity intact,
I must focus on something different
and ignore the simple fact –

We need a miracle.

And the guilt that I am feeling –
is it because I have lost hope?
Or simply that I am tired
and find it difficult to cope?
But hope is what keeps us going –
without it, we are lost.
So, I must dig deep into my pockets,
(never mind the cost)
and buy the pipe dream.

# what is hope?

We whisper it in prayers –
are they listening?

We offer it as comfort –
is it helping?

We write in a card –
to give it meaning.

As if it's something real –
are we dreaming?

Is hope a wish, a whim?
Is hope a flight of fancy?
Is hope romantic notion?
Is hope the gift, we cannot see?

Hope is nothing tangible,
it's not a thing to give away.
Hope does not exist
within the platitudes we say.

So – what is hope?

Hope is bruises.
Hope is blood.
Hope is crawling on all fours.
Hope is picking yourself up.
Hope is fighting for what's yours.

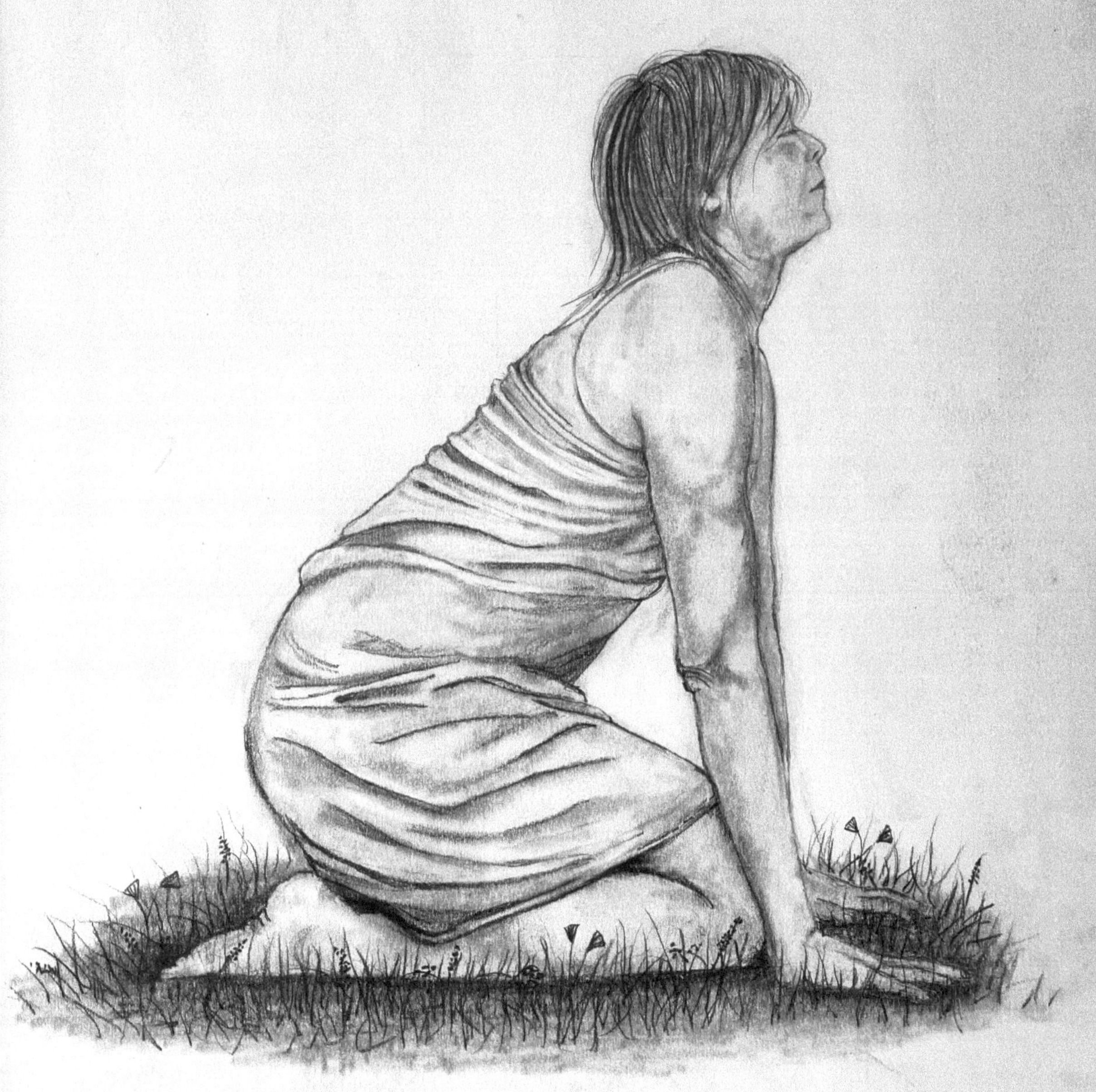

Hope is laughing at your troubles.
Hope is facing all your fears.
Hope is staring in the mirror.
Hope is wiping away tears.

Hope is looking at your half-filled cup
and saying that it's full.
Hope is all you are.
Hope is an iron will.

Hope is what we offer
when there is nothing left to give.
But we already have it,
when we choose to live.

# angel

This morning – I thought I saw an angel
just a glimpse,
out of the corner of my eye.
She passed by my kitchen window
shimmering in early morning sunshine
while I washed dishes.

By the time I looked up
she had gone.
But I thought
as the soapy bubbles glistened iridescent,
'How nice it must feel,
to be the bearer of good things
on such a beautiful day.'

And even though I know
she wasn't really there –
I can choose to believe if I want to.
And who doesn't want to believe in angels?

*(This poem also appears in 'Out of the Blue' an anthology of Poems published by Parkinson's Art)*

# five little words

*"I can do hard things"*
These are my gift to you
just five little words
to help you see things through.
Never to be forgotten,
*"I can do hard things".*
These five little words
are words to give you wings.

When the mountains feel too high
and the rivers run too fast,
when the oceans are too wide
and the deserts – all too vast.
When the problems seem so big
they are impossibly absurd,
that's when you must return
to these five little words.

*"I can do hard things"*
will give you all the strength you need,
these five little words
will provide the courage to succeed.
*"I can do hard things"*
are enough to fill your cup,
these five little words
will stop you giving up.

Five little words
worth their weight in gold,
five little words,
that never will grow old.
So if you're looking for advice
to deal with what life brings
take these five little words
***"I can do hard things.***"

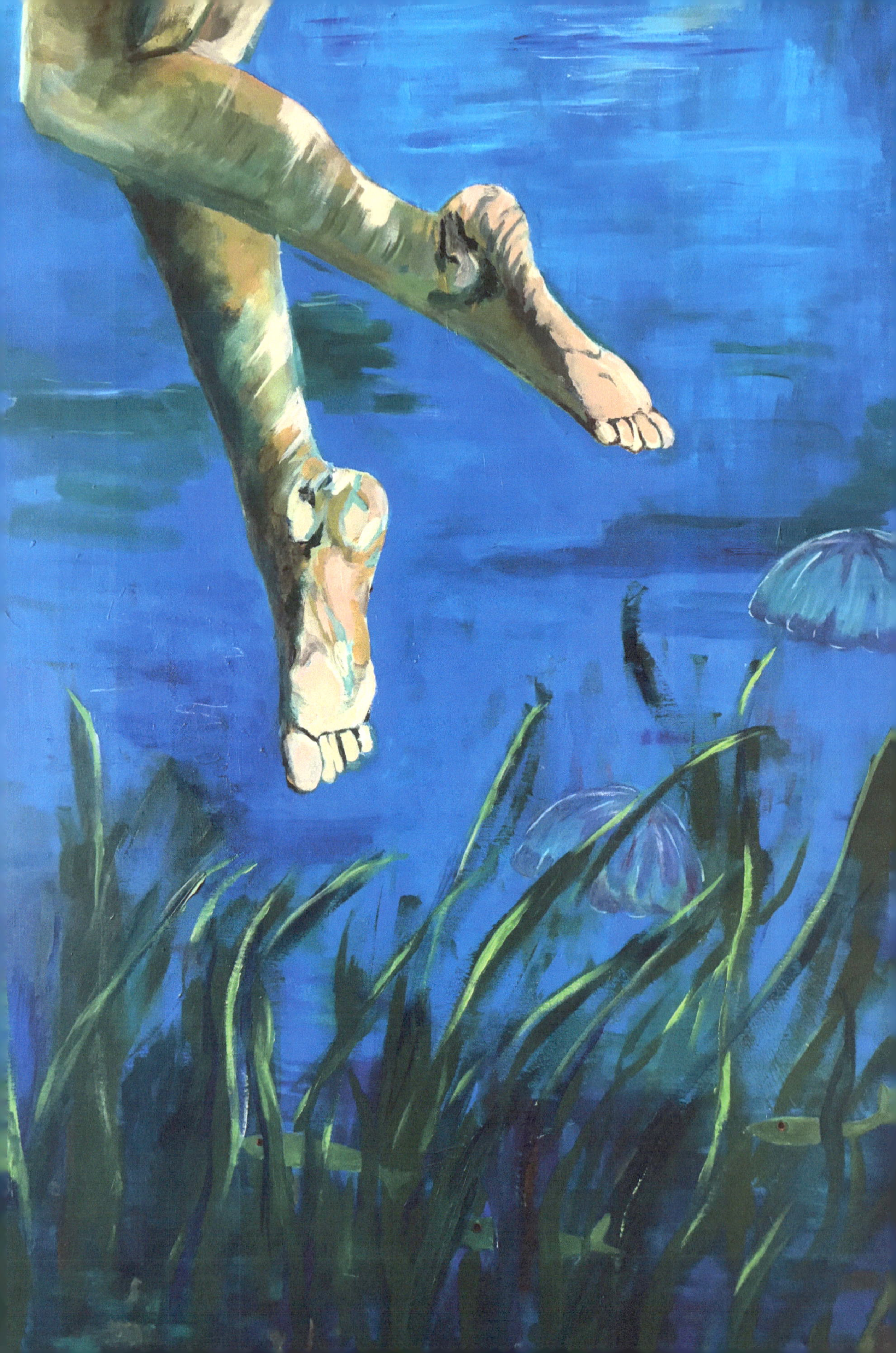

# super-hero quality

I realise I have become a 'cliché' as I am walking to the sea,
a slightly older woman wanting to be free,
seeking some enlightenment, some respite or escape,
a 'renewal' that will spur me on and force my soul to wake.

And as the waves rush over, my already frozen feet,
"Ooh it's cold today!" the same phrases I repeat,
as if it would be any different from the day before
and I wonder what it's doing, to keep me wanting more.

But still, I keep on walking deeper – whilst making operatic noise
and I lift my arms up high, with almost balletic poise.
It's a reflex as my body seeks its own escape
from the water rushing around me like an icy cape.

Then as I gather all my courage to dive beneath the tide,
I ignore the choppy water that's chilling me inside.
It's time to chant my mantra softly in my head,
"I can do hard things" I feel better once it's said.

And then suddenly – the tingle – hard to describe in words,
a prickle flowing over skin it really sounds absurd –
an elemental force that comes from deep within,
that banishes the cold, like holy water washing sin.

Then as I break the surface once more to face the dawn,
I am swimming into sunbeams and I have been reborn.
I don't care how others see me when I'm walking from the sea,
I'm now a slightly older woman – with super-hero quality.

# lighter than a bird

I used to be light – like a bird, hollow-boned and free,
to dip and dive and soar, turn somersaults and surf the breeze.
But now my hollow bones feel heavy, so dense they weigh me down
and every day it's harder, for me to leave the ground.

So, when my senses feel the ripples of the wind,
calling me to fly away, I'll try to lift my heavy limbs.
But even though my body, knows what it needs to do
nothing seems to happen, it's like I'm stuck with glue.

So now all I have are memories of when I used to fly
I have to close my eyes and dream, if I want to reach the sky.
But if I really concentrate, I can feel my stomach roll
and with every swan dive I imagine I move closer to my goal.

Until finally I break free, if only in my mind
and soar into the sky, released from the bonds that bind.
Lighter than a bird, surfing on the breeze,
I remember how to fly, hollow-boned and free.

# my mountain – North Berwick Law

This is my mountain,
it's different from the rest.
Rising from the fields,
I use it as my test.

This my mountain
less than 200 metres high
but when I reach its summit
I feel I can touch the sky.

This is my mountain
it's both my haven and safe place,
it's where I go for answers
ask for help or seek escape.

This is my mountain
where I go to for strength and courage
for wisdom and for faith,
so I will not become discouraged.

North Berwick Law, my tiny mountain
here for a thousand years,
this volcanic plug of rock
helps me climb away my fears.

# what will tomorrow bring?

What will 'tomorrow' bring?
There are no guarantees.
Tomorrow does what it wants,
it doesn't try to please.

So best to make the most of now –
yes! – Right now! This very minute.
Treasure this present moment
and smile at someone in it.

I'll bet you've made their day.
I bet they've smiled right back at you.
Now in this present moment
they are happier too.

So don't worry about tomorrow.
We both know that it's fickle.
Best live in the here and now
and find someone to tickle.

# it's time to wear the big girl pants

It's time to wear the big girl pants
with ribbons, bows and frills.
It's time to never mind the milk
when it falls and spills.

It's time to have your cake and eat it
with a cherry on the top.
It's time to fire on all cylinders
and pull out all the stops.

It's time to step up to the plate
and knock it out the park.
It's time to pick the pencil up,
it's time to make your mark.

It's time to face the music,
it's time to sing and play.
It's time to trip the light fantastic
and dance the night away.

It's time to lie on the bed of roses
and never mind the thorns.
It's time to take a stick and poke it
and grab it by the horns.

It's time to fly in the face of danger
it's time to spread your wings.
Don't stop when Elvis leaves the building
or if the big fat lady sings.

It's time to sew a silver lining
into every cloud you see.
It's time to throw the shackles off
and let yourself be free.

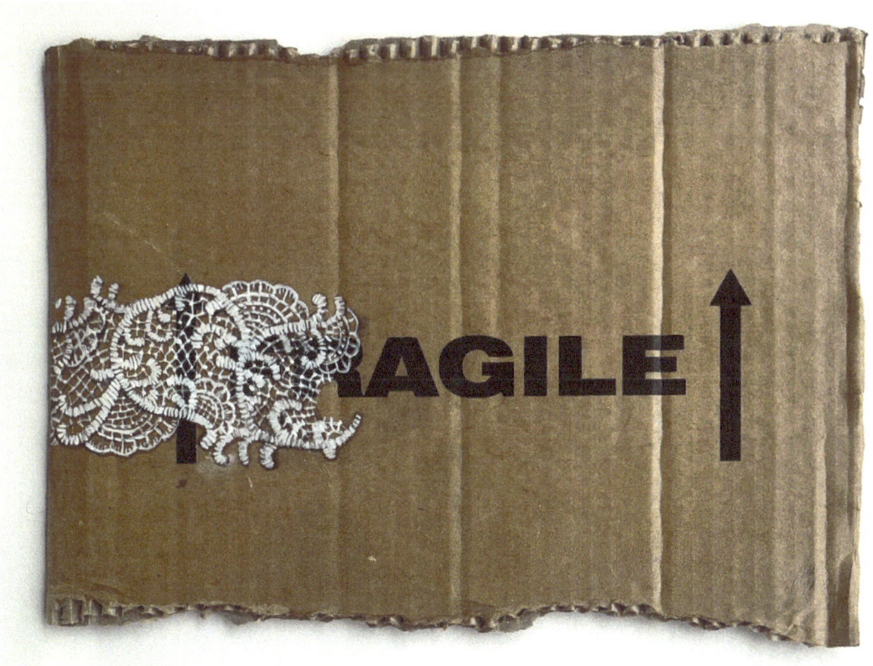

# the lost poem

It's the middle of the night
when the words fall out my head,
they are there when I wake up
it's as if my brain has bled –
all the lost and secret things
hidden in my mind,
the words I want to say
that in the light of day can't find.

But there is nothing I can do at night
except to try to write them down,
so, in the morning when I wake,
they can still be found.
But usually what happens,
is that, by the time I find my pen
they have disappeared completely,
and I have to start again.

Because those words – they are elusive
and they are never quite the same,
or as clever as I thought,
as when they fell out of my brain.
There is always something missing –
a random puzzle piece,
a slice of blue sky thinking
that made the words unique.

So, I return to bed frustrated,
awake, deprived of sleep,
wishing there was a way
to save the words I'd like to keep.
Make them stay inside my brain
and not fall out my head,
so they are still there in the morning
when I wake up in my bed.

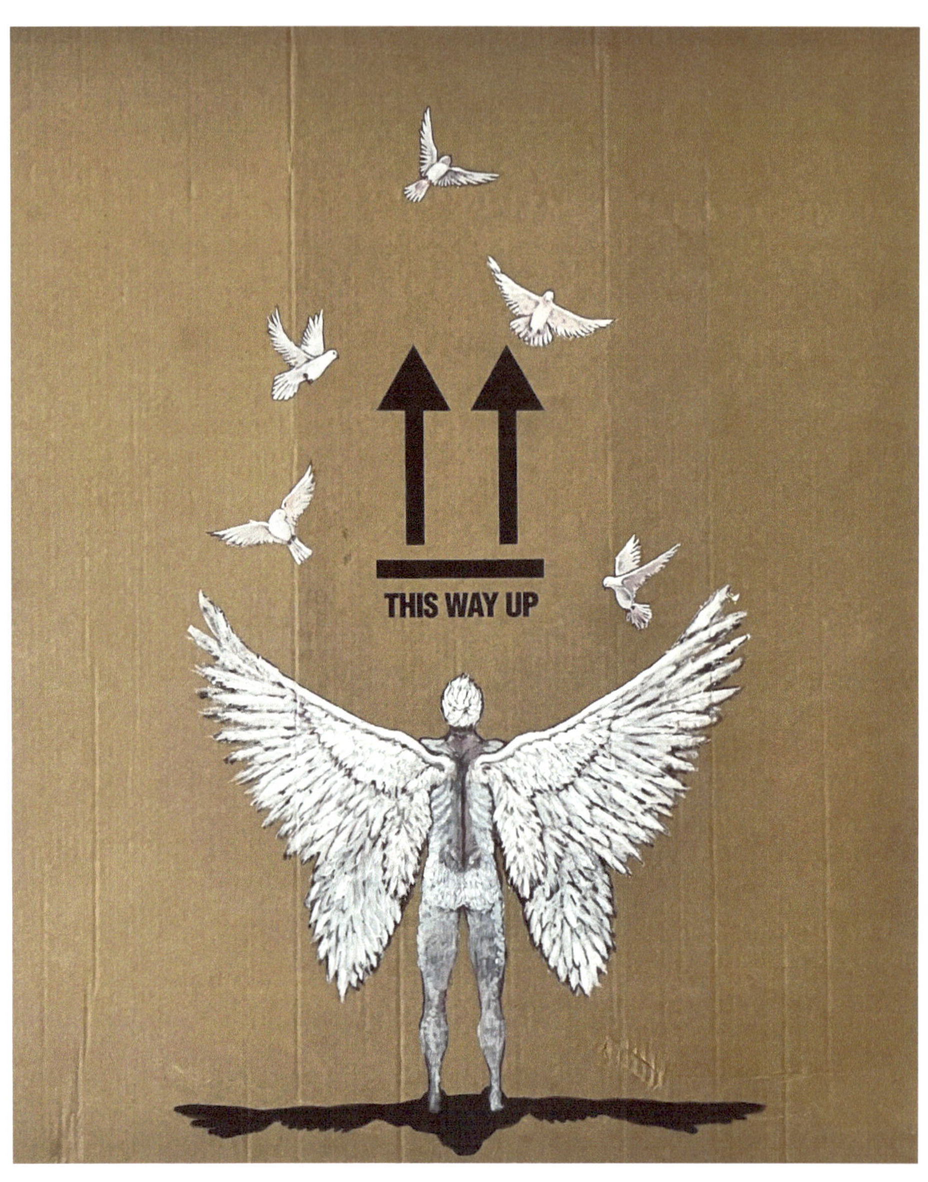
THIS WAY UP

# this way up

'This Way Up' – the writing is quite plain
but what does it really mean
because it's different in my brain.
'Put me upside down
and I could end up damaged'
but when I read those words
it conjures up a different image.
This time it was an angel – looking to the sky
I often think of angels,
I'm really not sure why.

# the last five minutes

I try hard not to be slow, I wish I could do more
I'd rather not be, last out of the door
but buttons fight back and zippers are worse,
shoelaces impossible, belt buckles a curse.

So now I allow – lots of time to get ready
for fingers that fumble and feet so unsteady
and I have a routine, to help things along
but it's in the final five minutes, things always go wrong.

The last five minutes are when things go awry
and no matter how organized, or how hard I try
there is always a 'something' that I need to do.
More often than not – it's a trip to the loo.

An 'emergency wee!' A panic of sorts.
'A just in case wee.' So, I don't get caught short.
And now I am rushing, I don't want to be late,
but really, I know – it's all up to fate.

Because the more that I panic, the slower I am.
And now it feels like I am moving through jam.
Next, it's the keys that get stuck in the lock.
I twist and I turn them but it's like they're in rock.

I need a 'King Arthur' to remove them for me.
Then after perhaps, he'll get down on one knee
and help to pick up all the stuff on the floor,
that dropped when I wrestled the keys out the door.

And the lesson to learn, from this mayhem created –
so you too are not – annoyed and frustrated.
You can take as much time, almost any amount –
but it's only the last five minutes that count.

## the conscious cuppa

Every time I go to fill the teapot,
I end up sloshing water!
It annoys my husband
and I know I really ought to
try to be more careful.
But it's not like I mean to do it,
it's not as if I pick the kettle up
and say, "I'm going to make a cup of tea
but first, you know what?
I think I'll pour hot water
over all the counter!"

There is a disconnect somewhere
between my brain and my body
I know it's Parkinson's –
maybe he doesn't.

But when I fill the teapot for the second time,
after I've put the teabags in,
I don't spill a drop.
I am conscious of it now.
So, if I'm conscious –
I can stop it from happening. Can't I?
But it's exhausting being permanently conscious;
conscious of talking more loudly –
conscious of sitting up straight –
conscious of lifting your feet –
conscious of swinging your arm –
conscious of remembering your pills –

And after all that bloody consciousness
I just want a cup of flippin' tea!

# the angel on my shoulder

The devil on my shoulder,
likes crisps and sweets and treats,
she quite likes biscuits too,
as much as she can eat.

The angel on my shoulder
shakes her head in great dismay,
she knows the devil's greedy
and is hard to chase away.

So, one day she offered a solution,
a choice of two boxes I could take
and told me that the first one
a healthy life would make.

The second box she said,
was filled with something else,
diabetes, heart disease,
and deteriorating health

Then the angel on my shoulder
asked which box I would choose.
I said the answer's easy,
'a healthy life', I cannot lose.

So, she gifted me the box
and I took a look inside,
it was filled with fruits and vegetables
of every shape and size.

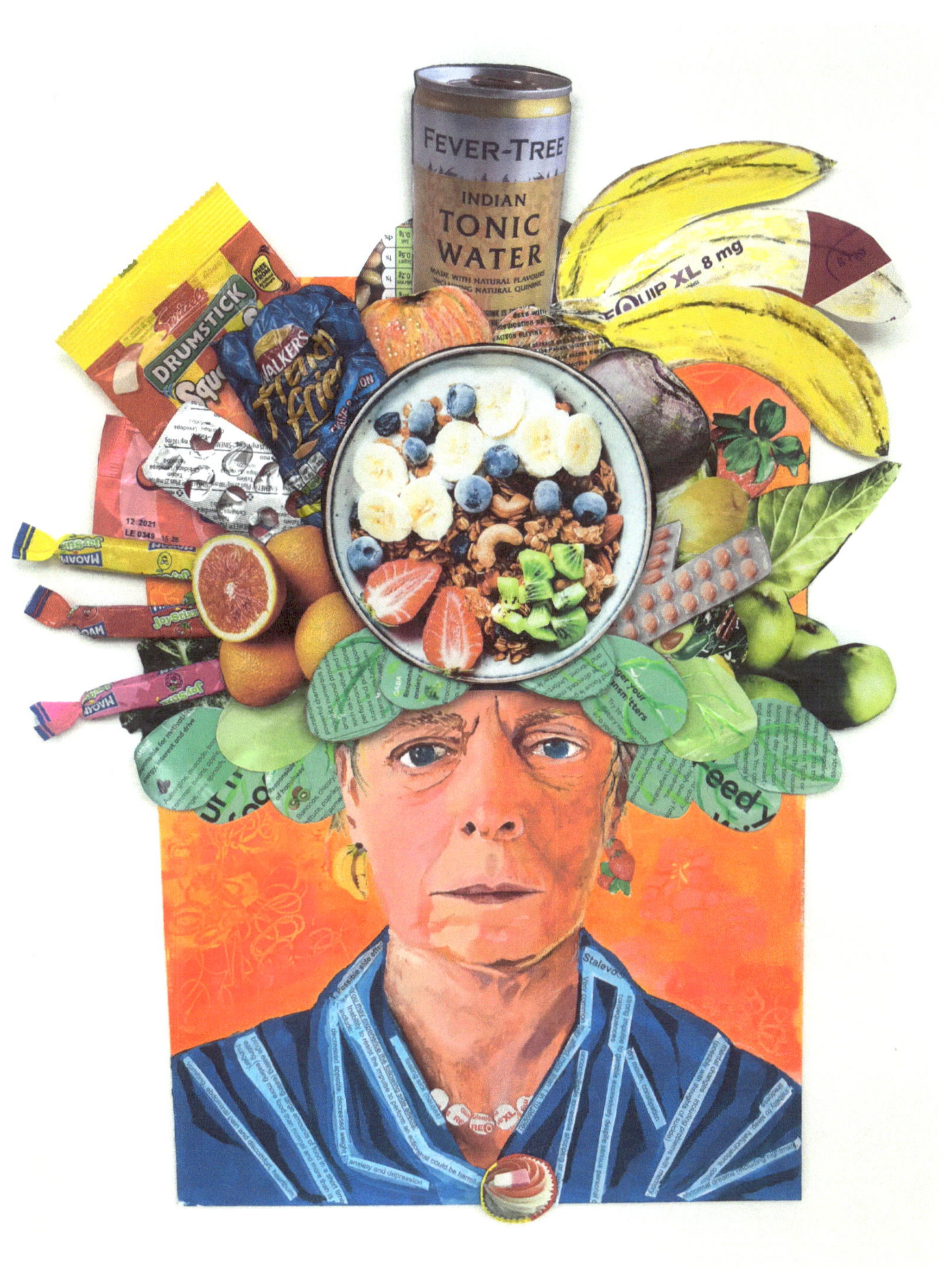
FEVER-TREE
INDIAN
TONIC
WATER
MADE WITH NATURAL FLAVOURS
DRUMSTICK
WALKERS
XL 8 mg

But the devil was not happy
and lifted up the other box,
tipped it upside down
and the contents out she knocked.

And all of my favourite treats
spilled out upon the floor,
chocolates, liquorice all-sorts,
Pringles and lots more.

Then the devil on my shoulder
started laughing greedily,
and I looked at the angel
and the angel looked at me.

Quick as a flash my angel
pushed the devil in the box
and I swiftly closed the lid
and then we both sat on the top.

And then I told the angel
what my mother used to say,
'A little of what you fancy,
will help you on your way.'

And together we both laughed,
then I offer her a Twix
but she was already tucking in,
to a bag of Pick and Mix.

# finding joy and peace in the sea

For Bernadette who loved to swim in the sea.

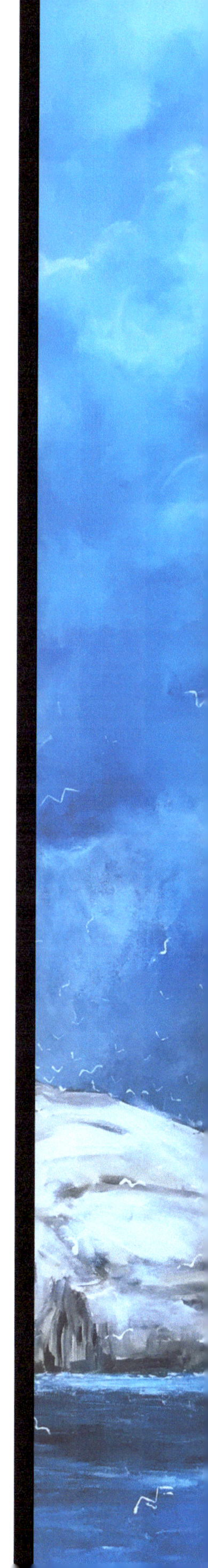

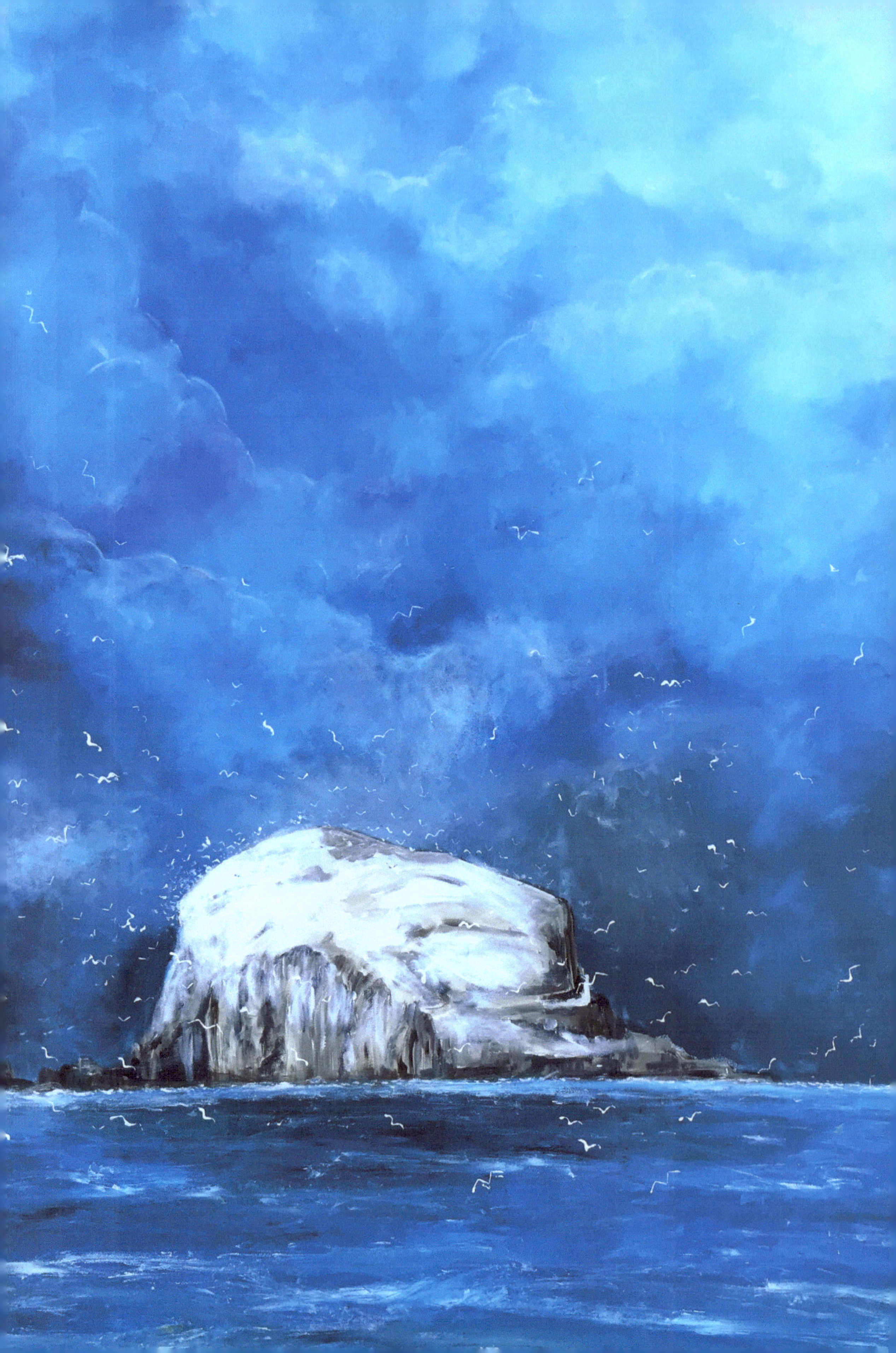

# the edge

I
like
to stand
at the edge,
where the water
laps over my toes and
threatens to wash my ankles.
I like to look across the waves to
the line of light created by the cusp
of the emerald sea and a cerulean-blue
sky and watch it shimmer like shattered glass.
I like to imagine I am wading towards that horizon,
pulling through the cold, salty water as icy chills inch
their way up my spine and send shivers through my body.
Then after breathing in deeply, I will sink deep, deep, deeper,
into the calm water beneath and watch silky, silver fish flit like
fireflies until I eventually have to rise and break the surface for air.

# floating

Beneath the waves
is the green water,
serene and calm,
seaweed swaying, fishes feeding
and the crabs.
I swim down, down, down . . .

Above the green water
is an azure sky,
vast and cool,
clouds surfing on the breeze
with the birds.
I fly up, up, up . . .

In between the green and the blue
is me – floating gently,
rising and falling
on the swell of a Spring tide
with the wild.
I let go, go, go . . .

# morning swim

I choose to swim in the morning
when the sun is waking,
creeping over the horizon
bringing warmth to the cold sand.

A necklace of lacy shells,
marks the turning of the tide,
limpets,
purple mussels,
periwinkles
and a piece of blue pottery worn smooth by the sea.
Its story is already written. I shall write mine today.
It will begin,

'Once upon a time, she dived into the ocean,'

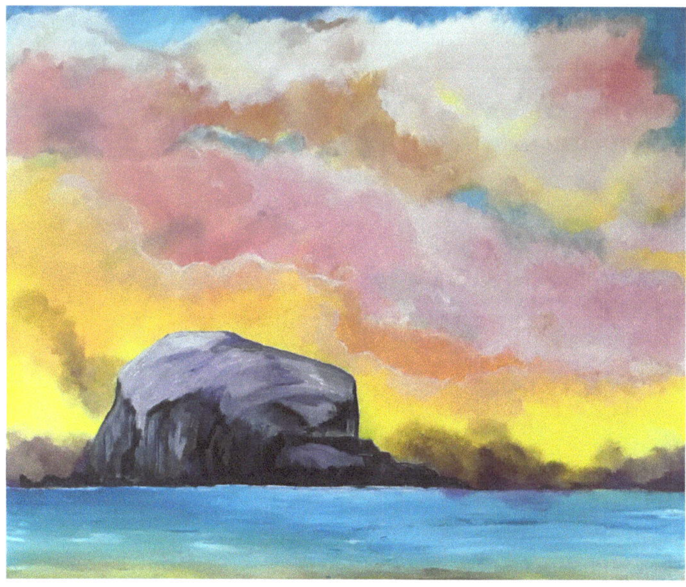

# swimming through sunbeams

It is Thursday,
The sun is shining,
The tide is high
and I am swimming through sunbeams.

Blinding beauty dancing on the water.
They are all I can see.

Guiding me with their loveliness to an inner peace.

# epilogue

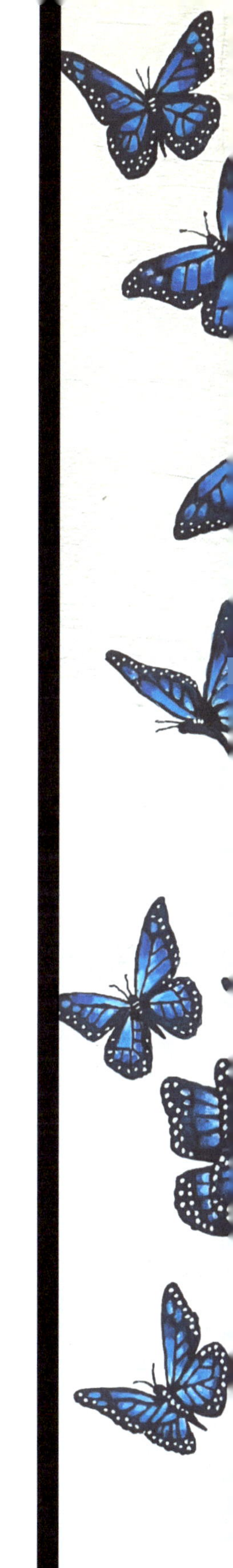

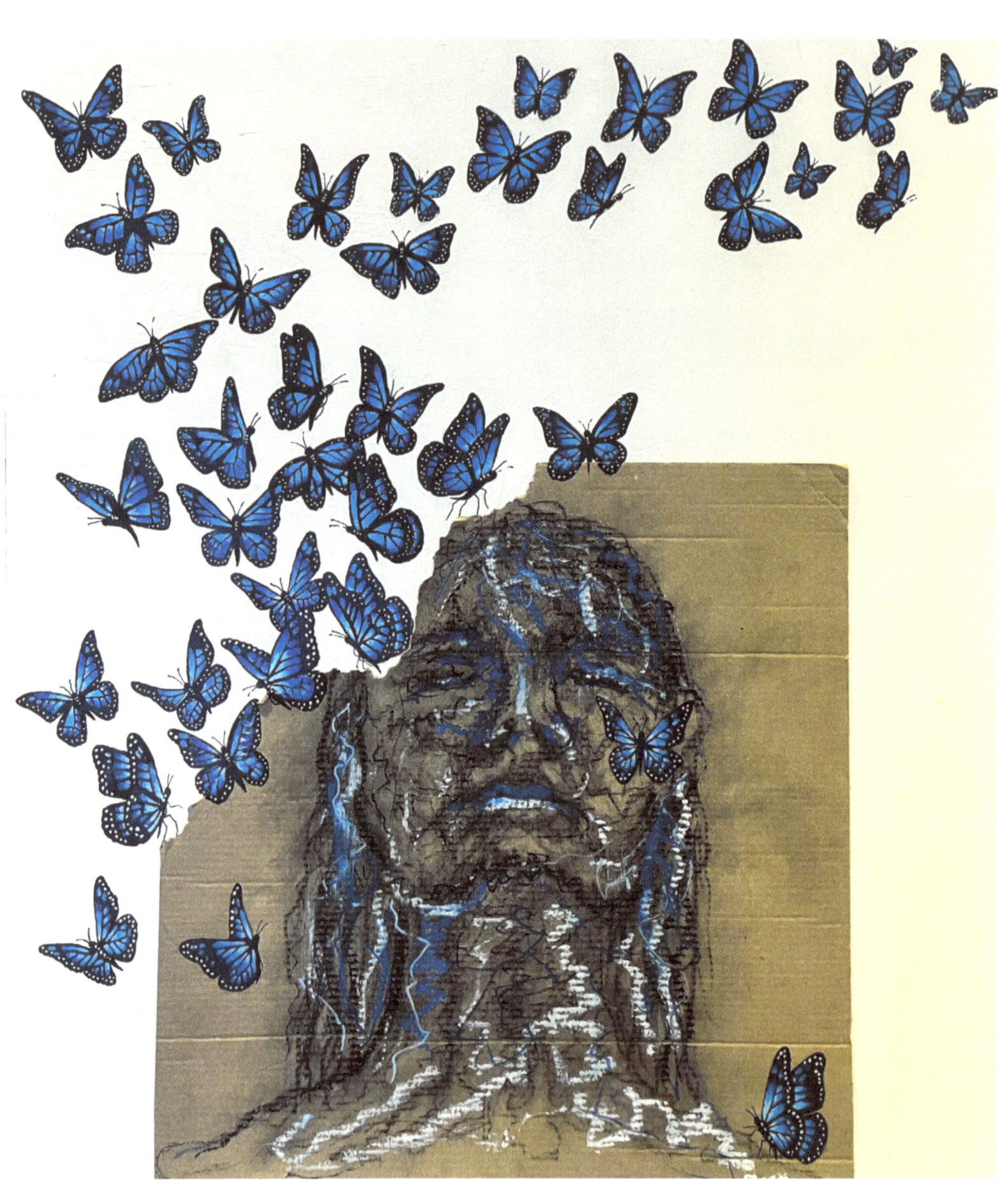

# when death comes

When death comes – I will welcome her with a song.

But until that day . . .
I will ring the bell and bang the drum.
I will stamp my feet and tap dance on the devil's back.

When death comes – I will welcome her with loving arms.

But until that day . . .
I will hug and kiss and cuddle babies.
I will stroke my lover's hair and surrender to the bliss of his touch.

When death comes – I will welcome her sweet peace.

But until that day . . .
I will scream and shout and gnash my teeth!
I will wail and cry and bellow the truth, I will not go quietly.

# afterword

Thank you for buying my book. I hope you enjoyed reading it, and even if you didn't, you can at least take away a warm fuzzy feeling because some of your hard-earned cash will be going to support 'Leuchie House National Respite Centre'.

# Leuchie House

Leuchie House is a national respite charity which provides transformational holidays for people living with neurological conditions such as MS, MND, stroke & Parkinson's, and helps carers and families have a break from caring responsibilities themselves. We believe the benefits of a holiday at Leuchie should go beyond the walls of Leuchie.

We provide 300 breaks a year at Leuchie and that tells us that a lot of people have unimaginably difficult lives and the number of people facing these challenges is growing.

Leuchie has been at the forefront of health and care for 60 years. Today we are delivering transformational breaks in a highly regulated environment, through our in-house neuro-experienced team of nurses, physiotherapists, occupational therapists, technology experts and carers. We are unique in the way we blend short breaks and services, and our care provision is recognised as exemplary by our regulator and guests.

Find out more about what we do, how we do it and how you can help, below.

**https://www.leuchiehouse.org.uk**

# acknowledgements

This was a project that started the day after my diagnosis; I am not sure I would have picked up a paintbrush or written a poem had I not developed Parkinson's. I also know this journey would not have been much harder had I not had the love and support of family and friends. With that in mind, I would like to thank the following people.

Dave Blevins – my long-suffering husband and one of the most patient and supportive humans on this planet, who never baulks at my crazy ideas.

My sons, you light up my world.

My sister and brother because you are there for me when I need you. Stephanie Blevins for your belief, encouragement, and support.

My friends, there are so many of you, but special thanks to: Saartje Drijver, Marion Wightman, Patricia Gibb, Lindsey Robb, Joan Lunn, and Mary Higgins.

Emma Bell and Alisoun Mackenzie for your advice, encouragement, and absolute faith that I could do this.

My fellow 'The Art of The Possible' artists Nicky Stannage, Nat Spring and Bernadette Petrie.

All the poets at 'The Wall' – their enthusiasm continues to amaze and inspire me. The admin team Martin Pickard, Nigel Smith, Keith Trayling, and William Stafford – for your dedication and good humour.

Finally, to my sponsors, thank you all. Your donation no matter how large or small, helped to get this published.

www.ingramcontent.com/pod-product-compliance
Lightning Source LLC
LaVergne TN
LVHW070218110826
845147LV00003B/598

* 9 7 8 1 9 1 7 3 2 9 8 8 0 *